PENGUIN BOOKS

# Swell

Maria Ferguson is a writer and performer. Her poetry has been widely published and anthologized, and her debut collection, *Alright, Girl?* (Burning Eye, 2020), was Highly Commended in the Forward Prizes. On the stage, her one-woman show *Fat Girls Don't Dance* (Oberon, 2017) won the Saboteur Award for Best Spoken Word Show, and *Essex Girl* (Oberon, 2019) was shortlisted for the Tony Craze Award and won Show of the Week at VAULT Festival. She has been commissioned by the Royal Academy of Arts, *Stylist* magazine and BBC Radio. She currently lives in Leeds.

# MARIA FERGUSON

## Swell

PENGUIN BOOKS

PENGUIN BOOKS

UK | USA | Canada | Ireland | Australia
India | New Zealand | South Africa

Penguin Books is part of the Penguin Random House group of companies
whose addresses can be found at global.penguinrandomhouse.com

Penguin Books, Penguin Random House UK,
One Embassy Gardens, 8 Viaduct Gardens, London SW11 7BW

penguin.co.uk

First published 2025

002

Set in 10/13.75pt Warnock Pro
Typeset by Jouve (UK), Milton Keynes
Printed and bound in Great Britain by Clays Ltd, Elcograf S.p.A.

The authorized representative in the EEA is Penguin Random House Ireland,
Morrison Chambers, 32 Nassau Street, Dublin D02 YH68

A CIP catalogue record for this book is available from the British Library

ISBN: 978–1–802–06435–3

For Rory

# CONTENTS

Lambing Season     1

## I. WOOD-CHIP

Ceiling     5

I Read Somewhere You Should Start with Plants     6

Leading the Mother and Baby Group     7

Serrated     8

History     9

There's a Woman with a Baby in the Local Café     10

Lil-Lets Smart Fit Applicator Tampons     11

Valentine's Day     12

On Honeymoon I Dream of My Abuser     13

Reunion     14

Anxiety Sneaks In Through the Window One October     15

Scare     16

The Conversation     17

I See Him with His Kids at the Local Park     18

I Didn't Think I'd be Able to Buy a House     19

Springfield Road     20

Stay with Me OK Stay with Me     21

## II. NESTING

| | |
|---|---:|
| Voyeurism | 25 |
| North–South Divide | 26 |
| Newlands | 27 |
| So Much Can Change in Three Minutes | 28 |
| Pomegranate | 29 |
| The Waiting Room was Purple | 31 |
| Nesting | 32 |
| And Yet On Some Nights | 33 |
| I Didn't Get to Say Goodbye, I Barely Said Hello | 35 |
| I Am All the Things I Think I Should Be | 36 |
| Is It the Fault of the Vessel, Then? | 37 |
| I've Been Getting to Know My Cervix | 38 |
| Breakdown | 39 |
| Six Months Married | 40 |
| Maybe I Should Plant a Seed | 41 |

## III. SWELL

| | |
|---|---:|
| Sex May Feel Different When Trying to Conceive | 45 |
| Interlude | 46 |
| Party | 47 |
| If You Crave Dust, Concrete or Bricks Contact Your Midwife Immediately | 48 |
| Two Pink Lines Do Not a Baby Make | 49 |
| Twelve Weeks | 50 |

Endurance                                              51

Bombs are Falling, But Not Here                        52

I Joke that More People Have Seen My Bare
    Stomach in Pregnancy than in the Rest of My
    Life Combined                                      53

Intimacy                                               55

The Sonographer Says He Has My Nose                    56

Full-Term                                              57

Aslan is On the Move                                   58

## IV. INDIGO

White Noise                                            63

In Your First Weeks I was a Baby Too                   64

A Letter to My Husband from the Northumbrian
    Coast                                              65

Forgive Me, Sweetheart                                 66

Inside the Mother and Baby Group                       67

Harry Styles Just Won Four BRITS                       68

Your Libido May Suffer Postpartum                      70

Supernova                                              71

Notes on Our Marriage                                  72

I Think My Ten-Month-Old Might be Completely
    Indifferent Towards Me                             73

Inferential Statistics                                 74

Now That You're Living Everything's Dead               76

Gypsophila                                             77

Some Days We are Perfect                               78

You are My Sunshine      79

I Take My Toddler Out for Dinner      80

Bamboo      81

*Notes*      83

*Acknowledgements*      85

## Lambing Season

As usual the cuts of meat hung cocked
in the butcher's window.
Elderly women came for their sausages.
Lamb hearts for the dogs.
A new coffee shop had opened up
on the high street, serving
a shamelessly similar menu to the one
a few doors down.
Never before had I felt such air.
The evenings were periwinkle.
I was sober. Freckled. Loved.
Every so often, a slight whiff of petrol.
I didn't complain. How could I?
When the coffee was served with such flourish!
When I lost that first pregnancy it was
deliciously warm. The sun beat down
on the canal like it had something to prove.
I glugged it down. Pints of it.
Blocks of yellow butter.
Children in Easter hats.

# I. WOOD-CHIP

## Ceiling

I screamed your name as water gushed
through the light fittings. You banged

our landlord's door. He lived above,
was cooking for his family.

Complimented the smell of the chicken,
said his pasta bake felt boring. That water

the whole time, pouring.
You spoke to him about guttering.

I imagined myself as your wife.
Cooking for you in a house

in the country. A garden, a gate, a ceiling
that would hold. I thought of voices

in the house. Fish fingers
on Fridays. Drawings on the fridge.

The rain eased to a gentle tap.
You mopped. I finished. Forgot the stuffing.

Some days I want you to come inside me
just to see what happens.

## I Read Somewhere You Should Start with Plants

I eat my breakfast as usual. Bowl of granola,
oat milk, black coffee, spill a few drops
down my dressing gown. I've been having trouble
sleeping. Putting my clothes on back to front,
leaving my keys in the fridge. I drop my phone
down the loo, flush and light a match.
Sit on the edge of the bath and think
of all the times I've been caught masturbating.
I try my best to stay calm, reverse the damage.
Think maybe a drink would help. A different room?
It's still dead. A rotting on the windowsill.

## Leading the Mother and Baby Group

Wednesday mornings. Bethnal Green.
Cushions in primary colours.

*He-llo Tabatha*
*He-llo Clemmie*
*He-llo Joc*

The babies gurgle in dungarees.
Tiny designer shoes.

*The wheels on the bus go round and round . . .*

They eat their fists. I smile as I sing.

*Do you know any songs in Japanese?*

I read *Peepo*.
Tin baths and dad in a vest.

*Maybe next week we could count in French?*

I wave bye-bye to every child.

*Bye-bye, bye-bye, bye-bye*

The mothers wrestle bulging satchels,
grapple with coffees, nappies, wipes.
The babies squawk in unison.

I lift off,

                    weightless.

## Serrated

I'm a brat.
Raising my voice after glass three.
Honestly, who do I think I am?
Swanning about in my garish jumper.
Might as well have whacked Grandad
round the bonce with a sodding brick!
I've started the second layer of choccies
before the top one's done, dear God,
I've gifted you the wrong bread knife.
The *Eastenders* drums kick in.
Just look at me. Spilling gravy
all over the bloody carpet.
Jesus wept. See what I've done?
Mum's burning cinnamon candles,
adjusting the crib and crossing herself.
I'm a heathen. Bleating sheep.
Dad shakes his head, the queen rattles on.
I crack an inappropriate joke,
look around for some kind of offering:
that grandchild they've always wanted,
bread and butter pudding as good as nan's,
a mortgage, the right type of knife.

## History

Our mums worked together,
teaching at a primary school.

We spent afternoons cutting sugar paper.
Pritt-Sticking work for displays.

They drank coffee, wrote jokey poems
slagging off the head and cackled

through adjoining classrooms. We rolled our eyes.
Snuck chocolates from their cupboards.

I watch you now, my best friend,
lifting your daughter out of the swings.

Gently shaking her tiny body as if loose change
might jangle from her miniature parka.

You are brimming with life, your toddler nuzzled
into a bump that's just starting to show.

Your mum's been moved to a hospice. And now
mine plans her own funeral every time she drinks.

## There's a Woman with a Baby in the Local Café

Peroxide hair, shaggy and cropped, effortless.
Tattoos of naked women up her arms.
She drinks her iced latte through a straw, laughs,
son gurgling away on her hip.
The kind of woman who has her own paintings
in her boldly decorated living room,
a kitchen island, self-respect.
Is this the part where she turns her head
and we realise that she is – plot twist – me?
No. I watch, with my cinnamon bun.
Moisturiser in both eyes. My flat, falling to bits.

## Lil-Lets Smart Fit Applicator Tampons

*Expand all the way round*

What exactly
is coming
        out of me?

*Less packaging, less WASTE*

I have taken
the morning
after pill
more times
than I
can remember

*We're honest and we'd like you to be too*

I can't believe I'm thirty
                    one

*If you've got questions or need some advice*

I'm carrying rocks in my lower back
Holding my tits going up and down stairs

*Designed by women, for women*

I'm doubled over
                descending
                    terrified
                        of my womb

## Valentine's Day

Just look at me!
Exposing my stomach
in my own front room,
steak sizzling away in the pan.
It's delicious, isn't it?
I'm a bad bitch, baby! I DGAF!
Turning sideways and sucking in,
FUPA poking out of my lace,
hating myself at 3am.
I deserved that starter.
It's hashtag self-care.
Stop crying next to the microwave!
ASOS stocks to a 26.
You were miserable, weren't you,
when you were thin?
Picture cholesterol clogging my veins.
Just have a sliver, a slice, the lot.
Bin your jeans, wait for the likes.
You should be happy now, sweetheart.
A man has bought you a ring!
Why, then, are you so full up
with all these things you can't be?
Satisfied pop of a champagne cork.
Cigarette burning itself to the butt.
The clouds, unloading themselves.

## On Honeymoon I Dream of My Abuser

I pass him in the corridor and I want him
to want me. I've rolled up my skirt,
padded my bra. He teaches a class
on cadences; I suck the end of a pen.
He has a wife. Two kids.
He tries to resist, but it's futile, really,
the way I'm flinging my young body
all over the practice rooms.
When he corners me on the last day of term
I don't know what to do
except press a lime-green folder to my chest,
back myself up against the wall as he comes
towards me, clear as cold water – and I gasp
through the surface to a man's touch,
eggs and coffee, a Highland view.
I am thirty-two. A wife. Married
to a man who works in schools
where the girls giggle at break.

## Reunion

These days, we have husbands,
functioning drink problems, jobs, children.

We drink our wine in the entrance hall
like it's a set-up, headmistress

about to bound through the doors –
*What do you think you're doing, ladies?*

Make-up remover and wipes in hand. *Put those down
immediately and get that muck off your faces!*

She never appears. My old head of English sidles up.
*I've read your book*, she says with relish. Tilts her head.

We silently speculate on each other's salaries,
compare our ring fingers, reminisce.

I tell six different people in eight minutes,
*Oh. Ha-ha! Not me. I can barely look after myself!*

Ask after a girl I used to love. *You know the one.
Sort of mousey? Played netball for Essex. Wing attack.*

*Always eating strawberry laces. Come on!
We all got pissed on Jägerbombs at her 16th . . . remember?*

Miles away, in a seaside town I love but can't afford,
a woman bears down, ready to push.

When I see the announcement on Facebook
I will smell Red Bull. Recite her home number by heart.

## Anxiety Sneaks In Through
## the Window One October

Waits for me in the kitchen sink, eating
a toffee apple. *Careful,* I say, *your teeth.*
He bares a gummy cavern. Points to the fridge.

The following morning, I find him lurking
on top of the boiler cupboard, flicking a lighter
on and off with his pink tongue.

Sat in tepid, frothy water, thick
with coconut and lavender, I notice
one of the taps has an occasional drip.

By November he has taken to sleeping in my bed.
No funny business really, the odd spoon,
an occasional dry and awkward fuck.

We have a huge row on the doorstep.
Both of my wrists pinned to the frame.
I smell his breath, my insides stir. Heaven.

We part ways in late Spring. Share custody
of the white goods. On his visits we lie
on the kitchen lino, listening to them hum.

## Scare

I pray
for the first time
in years.
They cry next door.
They scream.
I contemplate a wailing
only I can soothe.
Feel my breasts swell
– would they leak?
Your hair thickens.
Feet get bigger.
Hands too. I imagine
growing round,
plump, useful
somehow – holy
fuck. Look
at the single line.
Discard. Forget
to flush.

## The Conversation

Half-drunk. Half-way through
the special meal you've cooked.
There are stains all over the walls,
an unpaid bill on the fridge.

As we masticate charred muscle
you ask how I would have felt
if the test was positive. Tears fall
onto my underdone oven chips.

You pour peppercorn sauce
from a giant Pyrex jug.
I pour more wine. A pea rolls
from my plate to the floor.

A house fly buzzes around the bins.
You want two. One of each.
I joke they would like you more
because you'd feed them rubbish.

*Can you cook us tea tonight, Daddy?*
I swill the idea with the last of the wine.
Notes of chocolate, red fruit,
the soft rolls of their necks.

## I See Him with His Kids at the Local Park

*after Marie Howe*

The one who got away –
coffee cup in hand, impeccably dressed
as always – and remember that Christmas
I returned to London, housemates still absent,
the place to myself. We tussled from front door
to bed, tripped over my suitcase still in the hall.
A button popped off his expensive shirt,
sailed across my rented room. I made a wish.
Its replacement is clumsy, to say the least.
Black thread instead of navy,
the button itself more cream than white.
How can he stand there so nonchalantly?
In that same shirt, that same body
I can no longer touch, drinking coffee
from a plastic cup in front of all these children.

## *I Didn't Think I'd be Able to Buy a House*

But now I know what you can get / the further /
and further / north / you go / I wonder if they'll
leave / the curtains / I push / for the garden shed /
lament the lack of period features / google *build
your own fireplace* / scream at my mum over video
call / beg / her not to die / within the next seven
years / inheritance tax is such a burden / I won't go
up that extra grand / that could buy me a fridge /
big american one / with a lever / miraculous ice

## Springfield Road

For five years I rented a room with stud walls
alongside two brothers, nothing alike
apart from the fact they were brothers
and their parents owned the house.
There was wood-chip in the kitchen,
a framed picture of Barry Manilow
in the shared living space.
One of them bought a part-Bengal cat
that would shit in the living room
when I had someone back for coffee.
I drank heavily most nights. Forgot who I was.
Someone would ask me for directions
outside the tube. I'd draw a blank.
Stare at *pain aux raisins*. Return home.
Sometimes slugs would appear
under the bay window. I'd peel them
from the plaster. Take them to bed.
Wake to find them buttoning a stiff, collared shirt.

## Stay with Me OK Stay with Me

Say it was my mum
not yours
we lost
that strange year
when everything
stopped
say it was her
funeral
that had to be
livestreamed
ok
say it was
my mum

and your mum
got the train
from the coast
sat in the pews
like my mum did
for yours
ok
say it was you
watching at home
watching me
give a eulogy
                    pregnant
is that right?

stay with me ok
I'm hosting the wake
saying goodbye

to your mum
by the stairs
so she can get back
to you
in the kitchen
mushroom risotto

                              or was it

chicken?

stay with me ok

she can be right

                 here

reaching

              feeling           your belly

         a kick

smiling

fetching the spoons

# II. NESTING

## Voyeurism

The high street is a catwalk
in this village and they've all turned out
for you, honey – just look at them
outside *JASPER'S* with their toasties,
on the terrace of the wine bar
like it's St Tropez.

And here I come, the new addition –
*up from* London*, don't you know!*
*Swans in and buys a house*
*people from round here can't stretch to.*
*Bragging in THE MILL café.*
*On about how cheap it were!*

*Honestly, these southerners!*
*Her husband's northern, mind.*

## North–South Divide

I say *bath* and he says, *sorry?*
Ask what he wants for dinner,
he checks his watch.
Busy myself with gravy.
A whippet appears from nowhere.
His hand up my blouse,
rough and calloused.
*Did you get a new hat?* I ask,
fingering the tweed.
He tells me again how his dad
was a miner. Repeats how many
died at Hillsborough.
*Justice for the . . . what was it?*
I'm lifted onto the counter.
The canary falls off its perch.
In the mirror, a sensible haircut.
A string of pearls.

## Newlands

I sleep right through the midday sun
and wake to coffee, pastries, the bath.
Something is tapping the back of my head.
Give me claret and bluebells, sea salt, his neck.

The radiators won't come on.
The new neighbour's a hoarder.
I watch them leave from behind thin curtains:
condensation blooms on the glass.

He tells me to *come down from there*,
rubs my feet, pours a drink,
shares his food when the menu has teeth.
*Put your hands on me.*

There's a plughole somewhere between my ribs
and the water's swirling. *Just put me to sleep.*
I'm a pig, a cockroach, gorgeous muck.
How long will I be this in love?

Life won't be the same here, no
but at least I have a garden.
Can I just get old and fat now, please?
Pot plants. Hot tub. Barbecue. Dog.

The light is coming, will it be enough?
To bob here, stupid as buoys.

## So Much Can Change in Three Minutes

We'd decided; one final summer-
time to explore our new middle-class life.
The renovated mills and local brewery.
Eight per-cent pints, guilt-free.

## Pomegranate

I brush my teeth and think of the pip
pluck my chin
        pip
scramble some eggs
      milk and butter
      so hungry
      must be
        pip
doesn't know me yet
but one day it might
hate me
as much as I hate myself
shake its head when I dance
in the kitchen
      drive a wedge
      between me
      and my friends
I'll struggle to hold
a conversation
won't sleep
      for fear
      of lilies
me           him
   pip
      money
space
     a dog
         might gobble it up
no more sunday morning lie ins
      pastries with the papers
        brunch

I put on an old pair of dungarees
pip rips them from crack to crotch
            wriggle in the permission of it
might just be the making of me
imagine    pip
confiding in me
I go outside      eat my greens
fizzy orange tablet
                  fitbit
take great pleasure in the strain
collect names
            from american dramas
peanut butter straight from the jar
practice cradling
abdomen
            cluck
thinking what colour to paint the lounge
an unmistakable twinge
            cracks my insides open
            on the lino
            like an egg
I watch television with my husband
                  hands in my lap

## The Waiting Room was Purple

Purple walls, purple tables,
purple canvases of purple
fields and perfect purple skies.
The reclining bed was purple
and the curtain, and the chair
for my husband holding himself
where I would be if I wasn't
naked from the waist down,
closing my eyes and wishing I had
all the things that may have made
a difference. Cupboard full of vitamins.
Lion-stamped eggs. Some kind of
sparkling elderflower muck
to drink on Friday nights.
In the consultation room I stared
at the purple flowers in their purple
vase and imagined my insides:
an ocean, a cave, a storm.
Purple pebble washed up on the shore
as a nurse passed me the booklet.
A word starting with M and ending in E
– like mirage. Like mistake. Like mine.

## Nesting

Look at mummy bird doing so well,
coming and going through that tiny hole.

I sit and watch on the kitchen floor,
mindlessly cramming crisp after crisp.

My dad thinks I'm too familiar
with my husband in his company.

I've been making people uncomfortable
with my constant crying and lingering hugs.

She comes hundreds of times a day,
pecks at the suet balls I've left.

They never detected a heartbeat.
But I'm still here in this new body.

This new life
with something missing.

Slugs are eating my dahlias.
The houseplants are wilting again.

I spend my days at the kitchen window
waiting for their first flight.

## And Yet On Some Nights

I think it humorous
to address him like an old friend.
*Sorry it's been a while, mate, you know how it is.*
And of course he does.

I always begin by thanking him
for my many blessings. A family who love me
mostly, good sex when I've had a drink,
my new cotton bedsheets.

I tell him about my sister's baby,
my friend's psychotic episode
and how I got a bit teary the other day
hanging washing on the line.

He knows all this too, of course,
though he never interrupts –
perhaps his most redeeming feature
and why I keep coming back.

I go on to apologise
for picking out the best bits of food
for myself when I cook
for my husband. For being jealous

of horrible things that have happened
to my friends
and for the life I made inside me
but couldn't convince to stay.

Then I ask him to bless my brother.
My sweet, sweet brother.
Awake on the other side
of our distance, counting his sheep.

## I Didn't Get to Say Goodbye,
## I Barely Said Hello

The cherry trees in the village only bloom for a few weeks
but that doesn't make it any less special.
It doesn't mean it might as well not have happened
or stop me from pausing to pose for a photo
in a matching pink tracksuit and show my teeth,
which I've always hated, and lift up my arms.
It doesn't stop me from smiling every time I pass
because they remind me it's spring and that the world
is still turning and I should probably call my mum.
I held my belly so tenderly. Went through colour charts, names.
Loved the idea of it so hard, I poured my wine down the sink.

## I Am All the Things I Think I Should Be

I rise early and walk five miles
before a bowl of Greek yogurt,
strawberries, honey
made by my own bees.
My dahlias are blooming
so beautifully, aren't they?
And look! I baked a lemon drizzle!
But I won't have any,
not even a crumb, not even a lick
of the back of the knife.
I cook for my husband in a little apron,
a pastel blue that brings out my eyes.
Feta, potatoes, walnuts and mint
in our south-facing garden,
one small glass of blush and my body
doesn't need the vitamin gummies,
quarter aspirin with my morning tea.
It just happens like it should, with no pain
and no bleeding, they just come
and I give them his name.

## Is It the Fault of the Vessel, Then?

When a ship goes down or an aeroplane crashes
into the side of a mountain;
the bottom falls out of your shopping bags,
milk and detergent all over the road.
The alcoholic gets liver failure.
An obese woman buckles at the knee.

I've never been one for a grand parade
though in the circumstances it might be nice
to have some sort of commemoration
besides the flush of a toilet cistern,
a soaked pad in a sanitary bin.
What I'm trying to say is

I'm lying awake, wondering
night after night if it's me. . .
and is it worse if I sleep rather well,
that I only cry when I've had a drink –
is it really the fault of the captain?
They always go down with it, don't they?

## I've Been Getting to Know My Cervix

Its mucus. Consistency, colour, position and shape.
Worry I'm not ovulating.
The birthdays keep on coming
and the pregnancies announce themselves
like hangovers.
I piss on a stick, study the lines.
One of my friends has a water birth
right in her front room.
I meet him four weeks later on a walk by the sea.
She says her hormones have made her stink.
I smell his head like in the films. Hold him close
as the wind picks up.
The waves in me are stirring and I'm waiting
for the flood. Every crimson splash in the porcelain,
every smudge on the paper, churning me up.
I obsess over my diet. Take evening primrose,
count my macros. They say that madness
is doing the same thing over and over and expecting
a different result. I'm a failure, a miracle,
battling my battered body.
Am I swimming or floating? Waving or drowning?
I track my flow. Run a bath. Hold myself in the foam.

## Breakdown

A red light appeared a hundred miles from home.
Pick 'n' mix fused in the heat.
Burnt rubber, giant strawberries,
an engine overwhelmed.

I had always imagined what it would be like.
Practised the *Oh Thank God!* Pictured riding
up front, worn leather, a man with a beard
and steel toecaps. Oil on his hands.

I counted five dead foxes and prayed
I wouldn't bleed through my shorts.
Planned a takeaway I wouldn't have to feel guilty about
until the morning. Kept my mouth shut.

It feels a long while since I've looked in the mirror
without adjusting my clothes,
or sang along to the radio
knowing all the words. I can't stop thinking

about how people feel entirely different things
and call it love. Search everywhere for my glasses
which are on my face. It rains
and I pretend to be terribly disappointed.

## Six Months Married

consider a dog / send a pink card / box of posh chocs /
swear I can feel it / quit red meat / spend eight quid
on folic acid / no lines / test invalid / I've used up my best /
pee of the day / salmon / broccoli / scandi drama / find
four more greys in the mirror / lie back and think of /
global warming /          / play out arguments on repeat /
it's 01.41 / and he's snoring so soundly / banging again /
from the woman next door / she screams at her kids /
rearranges the kitchen / sundays still belong to us / darling /
lamb just the right side of rare

## Maybe I Should Plant a Seed

Water it every day for a year
just to see if anything happens
and if it doesn't is it simply
the soil, the weather,
the worms? The flowers
they sent are starting to stink
and I can't bear to throw them away.

A tattoo then, maybe?
A feather in a box.
Some days I feel like I've made it up.
I sit with my back to the garden fence,
listening to the neighbours' girl
singing and playing alone with her ball,
wishing it into my hands.

# III. SWELL

## Sex May Feel Different
## When Trying to Conceive

*Where do you want these?* says Kevin
the delivery man, holding my underwear
in one hand and Bobby,
my childhood teddy, in the other.

I look for somewhere to put them and notice
three other men are building the room
around us. Fiddling with wires.

I realise I'm naked but it's not an issue.
Look down at my useless breasts,
my functional vagina.

I take Bobby and tell Kevin he can keep
the lingerie. He throws it out of the window
then lights a cigarette. We stand there
puffing away. The squeal of a saw.

## Interlude

I am waiting for the butter to soften
so I can bake a Victoria sponge.
The most I'd baked before this was a spud.

I have unanswered emails and unfinished pages
but my plants are alive and my bathroom
is sparkling. I want so badly to hug my mum.

An apple will not save me. Bread is not the villain.
This afternoon I will eat a slice of cake. Tomorrow
I might move my sofa and dance until I sweat.

My body is amazing. Spilling over
this bed, with nothing to do
but wait.

## Party

The lines appeared within seconds,
confirming what I already knew.
I sent a picture to my best friend
with the caption – *oh baby baby.*

Two days later I squeezed into a bundle
of tulle, held a glass of prop champagne.
My mum winked, drank both our shares
at dinner, couldn't stand. I danced

with my husband like we had no cares.
Every trip to the loo, a sigh of relief.
My auntie spilled red wine down my dress.
*It's nothing,* I said. And meant it.

## *If You Crave Dust, Concrete or Bricks*
## *Contact Your Midwife Immediately*

slice lemons and boil the kettle / consider
a teaspoon of peanut butter / stick to water /
cucumber / a cup of plum tomatoes halved /
by lunchtime I've cracked / on to the goodies /
stuffing gauze into my cheeks / glugging litres of
pop / sugar free / squash in a wine glass / to feel
like I'm drinking / sumptuous cramping / like butter
melting / except it's cabbage / wilted spinach / until
it's mars bars / scraps / from the chippy

## Two Pink Lines Do Not a Baby Make

Still I swear I can feel you in there.
Even though it's far too early – I know –
it feels like you're trying, little one.
It feels like you're trying to make me try
so I'm taking this opportunity
to say hello. To say well done. It's not easy –
any of what you've managed so far
and as much as I am so very wary
of comparing you to whatever fruit
you are likened to this week, believe me,
you are so wanted. So loved.
As much as I try not to picture you
it's all I ever do. I dream of my belly
full up with you. Of rubbing your head
so smugly in public. I practise on the sofa
at night while your dad does the washing up.

## Twelve Weeks

I'm still in bed at noon
half-eaten biscuit
on the bedside
most nights I dream
of bright red streaks
you place a hand
on my round belly
tap as if knocking
*anyone home?*
I'm trying to make it
around the park
wheezing leant up
against a tree and
*am I sick enough do you think?*
retching at the smell
of mince
*it's just you isn't it?*
waking up to say
*hello*
only most of the time
it feels like a trick
just a white rabbit
ready to kick
and we're holding
our breath
for the big finish
the wave
of the nurse's wand

## Endurance

If you go running along a certain track
and trip quite badly, graze your knees,
you think, silly me! What did I do wrong?
You think next time, next time I'll be
more careful. I'll slow down
or wear better shoes.
Rest up, be stronger.
Check the weather.
You think I'll lose a bit of weight
so it's not so hard to carry
this body and so you do
and set off with vigour, grateful
to be running again at all, and you make it
to the sonographer's room
holding your husband's hand as before
only this time, there's a blob with a flicker.
This time they show you the big screen,
start of the brain, a little hand. Dear God!
Can't you feel yourself falling?

## Bombs are Falling, But Not Here

Not yet. I watch a segment
on daytime telly. A maternity hospital
left in ruins and Holly is crying
over women in labour,
babies dragged from the debris,
while Phil is shaking, saying words like
*horrific* before introducing
the latest spring trends.

I cut them short – take myself for brunch.
Avocado on sourdough, chilli and lime.
I visit my nephew, play Polar Bear's Hiding,
eat sausage and mash with my sister
and her partner and moan
that I'm tired and I really miss wine.
Climb into bed with my affirmations, a husband
who loves me and works far too hard.

In the early hours I wake to kicking,
rub the skin you wriggle beneath.
You are so unaware
in your sac and your fluid, still growing,
still learning how to swallow and breathe.
I wish we could say that we didn't see it coming,
that the world was just fine
when we forced you to live.

## I Joke that More People Have Seen My Bare Stomach in Pregnancy than in the Rest of My Life Combined

Not to mention the hands

                          reaching

                                     inside me

*Relax*

                              *This may pinch*

          *Expect some light bleeding*

*Do you mind if I*

                  *just take    a quick look*

I brace

count on my fingers
my sexual partners
their names and the ways
they wooed me
their smells

I've been so careful
who I trust
with my body
since learning its worth
in the textbook way

(older man
position of power)

*Just let your knees drop*

        *down*

                *that's it*

the

        metal             jelly

           gloved fingers        are

    cold

but you take it
you must

        breathe

like they taught you

        submit

and unfurl
until you are

        open

exposing yourself
like that diagram
of a flower
you remember
from school

## Intimacy

When I think about it, tucking the label
back into my husband's shirt
is not that different from eating him
to survive on a desert island.

The musk of cologne as I go
straight for the neck. He doesn't flinch,
doesn't question why my hands
are coming towards him.

He's felt my skin on his skin
so many times before. Our little
tap on the back that says,
*I've got you. It's alright.*

## The Sonographer Says He Has My Nose

All I see is lumpy custard.
My mum says she sees my husband
in the custard and I think of crying statues
of Mary in places like Lindisfarne.
Most nights I wake in a cold sweat,
prod and poke so my stomach flips.
He's taking all my iron.
The supplements turn my poo black.
We've bought the pram, the furniture.
I think of my future while I do a light wash.
Allow myself jumpers as goalposts,
watching fireworks in bobble hats,
hot tomato soup. Sometimes I see myself
being wheeled around the ward, vacant
arms by my side. The childless woman
I've always envied has a book out
with a well-known press. She poses
with a hardback copy in the sun,
calls it her baby.

## Full-Term

I dig out a pair of dungarees
I wouldn't usually wear
because they show the curve of my belly
but that's what we want now isn't it, baby?
Push my stomach out a bit further
like when I was five, imagining this –
hands placed on lower back, waddling
like a fat duck – or later, when the very thought
made me want to unfasten myself,
step out jagged and new.
A man offers to carry my bags.
An older woman beams on the bus.
I spread across a double seat.
Devour a chocolate éclair.

## Aslan is On the Move

and POP
there it goes
the waters gush
through pads
and towels
and down
the stairs
and in
the car
the lift
the chair
the purple
waiting room

the midwife bands
belly tight
I swell
with the sound
of him
and I know
this is
my time
to breathe
and s u r g e
dig deep
and send him
d
o
w
n
and now

I'm my mother
birthing before
my mother
before
birthing me
my mother
who's always
done
her best
saturday stories
talking lion
broken magic
eggy bread

reminds me
of her
blind belief
her faith
               p u s h i n g
on
and forward
send five words
she'll understand

she'll know
          he's coming

# IV. INDIGO

## White Noise

I sleep naked, not for pleasure
but convenience, breasts seeping
onto the sheets. I pump in the dark
as my husband snores. We whisper
through dinner, a glass of wine, fuck
in the black, like my mother is in
the next room and we are just teenagers,
new to each other, my body undiscovered
in this foreign state and now
my days are just coffee and cake
and first time mums hiding their greys,
boasting their little one's sleeping through.
I'm crying in the bathroom again.
I'm lying awake as the white noise plays
and I wanted this. *I wanted this.*
I check his chest, feel it rise and fall. Feel
my naked stomach sag, how it hangs
from me like fruit on the vine.
He came a week early, sped up by a drip
and there was no doula, no breathing through,
just cables and beeping and needles and blood.
I'll never forget how he tumbled from me,
a cord that seemed to keep on coming
like a phone wire stretched up the stairs.

## In Your First Weeks I was a Baby Too

one minute I was in a hospital bed and then
a garden        a bath        a café
nothing made sense everyone just babbled
faces an inch away from mine
I couldn't see past my outstretched arm
and even then in black and white
I wet my nappies         sat in my stink
no one asked if I wanted to be touched or held
I was fed and clothed and shushed to sleep
bathed in gentle soaps        cried        didn't know
or care if it was day        or night
knew only        I needed my mum

## A Letter to My Husband
## from the Northumbrian Coast

Dearest,
I hope by now you've forgiven my absence.
I couldn't take the screaming. It was at least
a fortnight before I cleared the ringing in my ears.
By then I'd reached Berwick
and befriended a lighthouse keeper.
The waves have kept me occupied.
Cheese and pickle sandwiches.
Isn't there something darling about milk
being delivered? A pork-pie
wrapped in brown paper? The night I left
there were two mushy oranges in the bowl.
I could smell bleach.
Simon is an excellent teacher.
I help him bring in the boats.
We polish the lantern, sweep the stairs,
clear seaweed from the landing.
The past few nights I've looked out to the deep
and sworn I've seen a humpback whale
cresting the distant foam.
Do you think it's true what they say, my love?
That the days are long but the years are short?
I drink weak tea from a pewter mug. Pay attention
to the shipping forecast. Knit. I often dream
of those women in our village.
All neutral linen and bangled wrists.
How long has it been now, darling?
Can he tie his shoes? Does he sleep?

## *Forgive Me, Sweetheart*

I was bruised and torn up,
forgot how to sleep, threw covers
in search of your body, limp and blue
in my fever dream, I was a stranger
to myself in those weeks.
Felt like a failure, a let-down
balloon. Your daddy cooed
at you in his arms and I tried
so hard to feel it darling, that rush,
those waves lapping over my skin
but instead I was walking over pebbles
barefoot, pulling a hangnail steady
and slow, like a dog I drank
from the tap.

## Inside the Mother and Baby Group

They let me sit on the big blue chair:
the newest mother, sick
on her trackies, tired and tits out,
feeding her young.

Sticky fingers reach to the mouth
of the dungareed woman
reading *Oi Frog*,
oozing her sweetness like sap.

I have learned a new language
in these long, short weeks – hunger
and sleep cues and needing the park,
the light and new faces, dancing veg.

My son says *tired*
by rubbing his face, buries himself
in my pillowy breast.
I have been where she sits,

turning the pages, singing to babies
she sees once a week.
I remember so clearly
that feeling of pity

for women who lose themselves
for a year to a sentence of songs
on library floors. To playdates
with women they can't even stand.

## Harry Styles Just Won Four BRITS

I'm covered in yogurt blocking out the screams.
Harry Styles just won a Grammy.
I'm eating Crunchy Nut from the box
as he says *this doesn't happen to people like me.*

I google *Harry Styles age.* Harry Styles
is five years younger than me.
I'm starting to blame Harry Styles
for my postpartum anxiety.

I can't move for Harry Styles. Harry Styles
on *Lorraine*, on my Spotify playlist.
I imagine partying with Harry Styles
as I peg out a load of washing. Snorting coke

on the front row of a fancy awards ceremony.
And isn't it funny he's from this tiny village
in the North where he worked in a bakery
to help his mum, who he adores by the way.

Harry Styles is such a nice boy. He hugs
little old ladies. He wears collars and pearls.
Harry Styles doesn't lie awake, worried
he might be a terrible person who hasn't locked the back door.

Harry Styles is so hardworking.
He's been on tour for fourteen years
and forging a successful solo career
post-boyband is no mean feat.

Harry Styles could afford full-time childcare. Harry Styles
could pay off the mortgage. I bet Harry Styles
wouldn't let his kid bump their head twice in one day.
Harry Styles would definitely fit into pre-pregnancy jeans.

I think if my son dropped a toy in Aldi, Harry Styles
would pick it up. He wouldn't ask, *how's he sleeping?*
He'd buy me a cup of tea. Reach over the sweetener
to touch my cheek. *Don't worry*, he'd say. *He's thriving.*

## Your Libido May Suffer Postpartum

The woman at the café is moving her mouth
as if she were speaking. I have worn the same outfit
for the past four days. It doesn't matter what time it is,
it's always indigo in this house and a ship is always
about to leave, blasting its clamorous horn.
I speak, it has to be said, with an unparalleled eloquence.
I could go on for days about the beautiful strangeness
of the number thirty-nine. I can't remember
my postcode. Mum's middle name.
I never used to drink coffee, or dream in black and white.
These days people speak to me in a slightly higher register.
They think I haven't noticed.
It's always Tuesday. 3pm. Always a fan on full
in our room, making the curtains dance.
As soon as I reach the climax I second-guess myself.
Do I really deserve to be here? Did I bring a coat?

## *Supernova*

I'm calling my mum in tears again
from a house in a village that's supposed to be home,
where the mills are sourdough bakeries now
and the coffee is served with a leaf in the foam.

I haven't washed my hair in weeks. Feel like I'm failing,
afraid we're not bonding, that my milk isn't enough
to sustain him. My marriage is hanging by a thin muslin
blowing dry on the line.

Sometimes he smiles at me in the bath
and my world explodes like a star.

## Notes on Our Marriage

He never used to pass without touching my waist.
I used to wear red satin underneath my clothes.
Each day we grow more tired, fat, in love
with someone else.
In the mirror I see a burnt-out car
wrecked by a double-decker.
Smoke to ash in the layby.
Have another piece of cake.
There was a time I believed there was no one else
I could possibly share my life with. Ate him up
like a ripe fig. Today love is leaving him
in bed at 5am. Forcing spoon after spoon of mush
into a resistant mouth. When my son was born
I still thought I loved my husband most of all.
Then one day – bam. The bus hit.

## I Think My Ten-Month-Old Might be Completely Indifferent Towards Me

And I'm not sure if that's my fault or his.
It might just be his personality, or could be a result
of the number of times I've left him to cry in his cot.

When he was three days old he needed light therapy
for jaundice. He had to be kept under UV rays
for twelve hours. I couldn't hold him.

It took ten days to name my son. I ended up
calling him the same name I said the first time
I looked at his face. I didn't trust myself.

We have good times, sure. He smiles when I
stick out my tongue, blow a raspberry on his belly
but when I leave the room he laughs and laughs.

## Inferential Statistics

A woman sits alone at her kitchen table, tracing stars
into the wood with the tip of her index finger.
The front door slams. Her son stirs.
The neighbour's British shorthair cat
darts through the garden.
UK woodlands are home to over fifty per cent
of the world's bluebells, which then appear
on eighty-four per cent of white mothers' Instagrams.
Social media is killing our children.
A petition is calling for all nursery rhymes
to be banned with immediate effect. In a strange coincidence
the first four signatories are all women
named Charlotte. School cake is the best cake
especially with custard. It is normal
for breastfeeding women to crave sugar and starch.
A mother of three tells her friend over dinner
not to make any irrational decisions
especially regarding her relationship
while her son is still in nappies
and that she looks nice in her dress.
Holding hands is undoubtedly the most intimate act of love.
Research has found that as little as four hugs a day
can improve our life span. The longer the hug
the more blood pressure is lowered, and stress reduced.
Sleep deprivation has been used for centuries
as a means of interrogation.
The best piece of advice in any marriage is
don't go to bed on an argument
and always pay for the flatpack furniture

to be assembled professionally.
The woman is still at the table.
Her husband is four pints deep.
Their son sits up in his Ikea cot, waving to no one.

## Now That You're Living Everything's Dead

I've abandoned my plants
completely, poor loves.
The birds beg for scraps
at the kitchen door.
I turn my back, the radio up.
Picture the ways I could lose you
in seconds. Map my body
like a new lover.
That skin tag, just to the left
of my shoulder. Another right
on my knicker line chafes.
My hips ruin displays in shops.
I can't remember the word
*principles*, how to please
my husband or hold
my drink. Never thought
I'd somehow live to forget
how many pounds there are
to a stone or stand
on a stage and feel nothing –
but love, when I nurse you
in a public place I feel like God
must exist.

## Gypsophila

It is customary to gift new mothers
small white flowers.
A duck says quack. A cow says moo.
After I put my son to bed I revel
in taxidermy.
I don't know where I've put my keys.
I wish I could know how he feels
when I pick him up from nursery.
The playground packed with strangers,
a flash of my purple coat.
In a parallel universe I'm outside a taverna,
relishing terracotta, the finish
of a bold white. I don't know
if I'm a good mother.
I don't know why a pig says oink.
I don't know whose idea it was
to gift us yet another thing
we have to keep alive,
but I know the smell of his breath
when he's desperately fighting sleep.
The shape, the shade of my guilt.

## Some Days We are Perfect

Ethereal. Laughing in slow-motion
as we push him on the swings.
He naps. Sweet Jesus.
And I finally clean the bathroom.
Indulge in a chocolate digestive,
a hot cup of tea.
Some days we are serene with it.
Our love for this tiny body
toddling around in Velcro shoes.
We call Nanny and Daideo
and he claps his hands with glee
as they tell me what a good job
I'm doing. *He's lovely,* they say. *He's lovely.*
Some days he eats his broccoli,
blows me a kiss from the bath – my God,
he lets me wash his hair!
At bedtime he goes down easy
and we cuddle on the sofa
like we're not confetti strewn on a lawn
the day after a wedding. Like we're not
pulling muscles in our backs or forgetting
we're best friends. Some days
we are the people we pretend to be at parties.
Some days we kiss before bed.

## *You are My Sunshine*

When you go to bed, darling, I like to look at pictures of you
from months, years ago, even. How strange and fragile you are
in your vests with your gums and your cradle cap. My
little spring baby, bald old man, wriggling in the sunshine.
Looking at them now, my love, I barely remember my
pain. Not knowing how to dress you. Intense heat. Only
sleeping in hour slots, Daddy taking you, 6am, sunshine
stomping across my sad. All I wanted was to disappear but you
kept on needing me. Tits out in public to make
me feel haloed. Bountiful with milk. Daddy asks me
*do you regret it?* My answer always *not every day.* If you're happy
and you know it clap your hands. Nothing. When
daddy and I first met I was thin. If the skies
did their wet thing we stayed in bed. What are
baby bubbles, please? Pulling stitches. Burnt toast. Grey
matter continues to reduce for six years after childbirth. Lol. You'll
forgive me throwing myself a wake, right? I was never
convinced that it was for me and honestly? I still don't know.
No. Stop. Look at the pictures. My dear
little chicken, light of my life. But seriously, how
do I go on living with this rabid wolf in my chest? As much
as I question my carbon footprint, there are some days I
catch myself singing. You laugh. I think I might vomit from love.
At Sunday lunch, Grandma asks when I'm going to give you
a sibling. And yes, it has crossed my mind. But please!
My prolapse. Poor perineum. Endless, early difficult days. Don't
worry darling we're past it now. Sat here in our dungarees. Take
my word, oh hell. Take it all! My body, my guts, this kiss, my
forever. Beautiful boy. In the park. In the sunshine.
Waving a stick as big as your torso, shooing the birdies away.

## I Take My Toddler Out for Dinner

A fancy French place by the canal.
*Would you like to see the wine list?* I ask
and he says, *KADJADADADA,*
which means, *Absolutely.*
He starts aggressively banging his fist
over the Pinot Noir. *A fine choice, sir,*
the waiter bows, prising the list from his grip.

I order for both of us. Mussels to start
in garlic and cream, then seabass,
potatoes and samphire. In hindsight a white
would have been more appropriate
but no matter. I take my time buttering
the complimentary bread while my toddler
drops every piece of cutlery onto the tiled floor.

Each clang makes the woman at the next table flinch
into her bouillabaisse. *He's just so excited!* I beam
as he wipes his nose on the tablecloth and quacks.
The staff dance around us, expertly catching
each mussel shell mid-fall. Top up our glasses.
*SHAFAKAKAKADA BASHHHH*, says my toddler
which means, *This is delicious!*

Once his main has been adequately smushed
into the water jug, I take my toddler's hand.
*We should do this more often,* I tell him,
gently stroking his snot-crusted hair.
He agrees by loudly soiling himself
as the chocolate tart is served. The scent wafts
through the restaurant like blossom on the breeze.

## Bamboo

It sits there on the windowsill, doing its best
to live. The chicken defrosts in a white bowl.
The dishes are drying next to the sink, bananas
over-ripening, just the way I like. Glory be.

You are kicking a football around the garden
with your dad, pausing every now and then
to check that I'm still here. The radio plays
another song. I start to sing.

# NOTES

The italicized text in 'Lil-Lets Smart Fit Applicator Tampons' is taken directly from a box of the same tampons.

'I See Him with His Kids at the Local Park' is after Marie Howe's poem 'Separation'.

'Stay with Me OK Stay with Me' is in memory of Christina Carter.

The title 'And Yet On Some Nights' is taken from an Ilya Kaminski poem of the same name.

'Aslan is On the Move' is a quote from *The Lion, the Witch and the Wardrobe* by C. S. Lewis.

'You are My Sunshine' is a golden shovel, based on the lullaby.

'The Waiting Room was Purple' was Highly Commended in the Verve Poetry Festival Competition and appears in the 2022 anthology.

'Ceiling' was Commended in the Poets and Players Poetry Competition.

An early version of 'Springfield Road' was Highly Commended in the *Mslexia* Poetry Competition.

Early versions of 'Interlude' and 'Bamboo' were originally published by *Trapeze* in the poetry anthology *Everything is Going to be All Right*.

'Pomegranate' was shortlisted for the Outspoken Prize for Poetry in the Page category.

'I Didn't Get to Say Goodbye, I Barely Said Hello' came second in the Magma Poetry Competition: Editors' Prize.

'I've Been Getting to Know My Cervix' was commissioned by Experimental Words.

'Your Libido May Suffer Postpartum' was originally published as a finalist in the Montreal International Poetry Competition 2024.

10 to 20 per cent of known pregnancies end in miscarriage.

More than 1 in every 10 women and birthing people get post-natal depression within a year of giving birth. New fathers and partners can get post-natal depression too.

# ACKNOWLEDGEMENTS

With thanks to the following magazines, in which early versions of these poems appeared: *Perverse, Mslexia, bath magg, Magma, Butcher's Dog, The Poetry Review, The Rialto* and *The North.*

Thanks to The Poetry School, the Unislam Post-Emerging Cohort, the Out-Spoken Academy and Arts Council England, whose programmes and funding helped me to develop many of these poems.

Thanks to all the poets who helped with this collection, including Helen Mort, Jack Underwood, Caroline Bird, Cecilia Knapp, Toby Campion, Bryony Littlefair, Anthony Anaxagorou, Wayne Holloway-Smith, Talia Randall, Elisabeth Sennitt Clough and Alice Frecknall.

Thanks also to Salena Godden, Joelle Taylor, Kim Moore and Hollie McNish for their support and encouragement.

To my agent, Kirsty McLachlan, and everyone at Penguin Books. Thank you for believing in me.

To my Bosom Buddies – Jayne, Lucy, Laura, Claudia, Anna, Deborah and Catherine – and to all the volunteers at Bosom Buddies Pudsey. I could not have gotten through that first year without you.

To everyone at Mill Kitchen for the coffee and cake.

To Danielle for being a great friend and inspiration. Thank you for guiding me through those early days and beyond.

To Steph – my oldest and dearest friend. Thank you for allowing me to write your story as well as my own. I am in awe of you and your beautiful family.

To my son's many aunties, who continue to spoil us both.

To my family, who support me always, especially my mum.

To my brother, who we love and miss. I hope I make you proud.

To Matt, my husband and biggest cheerleader. I'm sorry for all I've put you through while writing this book. Thank you for being an incredible father to our son.

And finally, to our boy. You are everything I dreamed of and more. I am so proud to be your mum.